THE LITURGY REVIVED

THE
LITURGY
REVIVED

*A Doctrinal Commentary of the Conciliar
Constitution on the Liturgy*

REV. LOUIS BOUYER
of the Oratory

UNIVERSITY OF NOTRE DAME PRESS • 1964

Grateful acknowledgement is made to the publisher
of that translation of the Conciliar Constitution
on the Liturgy which has been employed by the
author of the present work. This translation
was published by the Liturgical Press,
copyrighted by the Order of St. Benedict, Inc.,
Collegeville, Minnesota

INTRODUCTION

THE CONCILIAR CONSTITUTION ON THE LITURGY HAS
planned a whole renewal of Catholic worship.
Such a renewal will remain as one of the most
striking religious events of the twentieth century.
However, this document gives us much more than
definite practical reforms. It embodies some underlying principles which reach even further than
any possible remodelling of the Christian liturgy.
These principles may well be considered as put-
ting the stamp of the supreme authority in the
Church (*C.J.C.*, can. 228) upon the main results
of the whole liturgical movement. They do not
merely, or first of all, touch the outward appearance of the worshipping Church. They are the
basic principles of the whole Christian spiritual-
ity, stated with a strength and lucidity no less re-
markable than the exceptional solemnity of their
utterance. Pope Pius XII had already done something along these lines in his famous encyclical
Mediator Dei. But the doctrine of the Conciliar

Constitution is much more elaborated, and is made explicit in a text which is not only a fatherly exhortation—however enhanced it may have been by the papal authority responsible for it— but a most solemn expression of the whole teaching Church. In the present case, all the Catholic bishops, one with Peter's successor, are seen exercising their extraordinary magisterium in its most authoritative form: *"Paulus, episcopus, servus servorum Dei, una cum Patribus concilii, ad perpetuam rei memoriam . . .* Paul, bishop, servant of the servants of God, together with the Fathers of the Council, for a perpetual remembrance of these things. . . ."* Here, we do not confront a *decree* on purely disciplinary problems, but a *constitution*, that is to say an irreformable statement of what the Church's belief is. Even, therefore, if no new definition of any specific detail of doctrine is involved, we find in this text a general declaration of what the Church, first of all, *means* by the liturgy. Such a doctrine can determine practical developments in the future other than those expressly formulated for today, and even on the doctrinal plane it may have to be supplemented in the future. But it will never be superseded as the Church's fundamental teaching concerning what she does in her worship. With that in mind, it will be understood that even if we mention here some of the major applications of the doctrine asserted by the Council, which have been pointed to as its natural consequences for the present time, it will be with this foremost object of making as clear as possible the doctrine itself. For this is the main objective of the Fathers.

It seems that their teaching may be conveniently summed up in five major points. The first ① is that the liturgy is the embodiment of the great mystery of our faith, source of all our spiritual life as Christians, i.e., what the Council calls the Paschal mystery of Christ, dying and rising again for our salvation. The second point, then, is that ② this mystery is properly the mystery of worship, not only because it is at the bottom of the worship of the Church, but because it makes of all her members those worshippers in Spirit and in truth that the Father was seeking. The third point ③ appears as a consequence of the second; the liturgical mystery is also the mystery of the Church, not only, again, because its proclamation to the world and its perpetual celebration is the great ministry committed to her care, her apostolic function, but also because it is the mystery of her own life, of her fusion into the mystical body of Christ Himself.

Next, we shall seek to discover the central role ④ which the liturgy is to play in the whole activity of the Church. The Council explains it as a summit towards which all the missionary activities of the Church are to lead, and at the same time as a source from which the whole Christian life is to flow.

⑤ Finally, we shall see how the Council makes plain that the liturgy, besides presenting the mystery to us objectively, in its sacramental embodiment, is intended to enhance our most effective reception of it: our subjective response to God's great gift of grace.

S.C. 14
Full, conscious, active participation

I

THE PASCHAL MYSTERY

THE CONCILIAR CONSTITUTION BEGINS WITH A PROCLAMA-
tion, the importance of which cannot be mini-
mized. In that proclamation, the Church endorses
one of the main contentions of the theologians
who have helped give the liturgical movement its
full significance. More especially, it represents the
best fruit of what has been achieved in the work
of pioneers like Dom Odo Casel and the whole
Maria-Laach school, which now receives its due
recognition. Of course, I do not intend to say that
all the details of what those religious thinkers
produced are now canonized. It should rather be
said that the supreme authority in the Church
has now distinguished, in the thinking of these
pioneers, the nucleus of undisputable truth from
hypotheses or mere personal opinions. However,
until quite recently, this nucleus itself was all too
commonly rejected, together with more or less
controversial representations. Even in the Council itself, voices were still heard which maintained
that to say that the liturgy is the mystery of salva-

tion proclaimed and now accomplished in us is meaningless: a vague and chimeric idea, dubiously orthodox, completely ignored by sound theology, and so on.

Now, in spite of those lingering oppositions or misunderstandings, the Council has decided to affirm, as the basis of its whole teaching on the liturgy: "[Christ the Lord] achieved His task principally by the Paschal Mystery of His blessed passion, resurrection from the dead, and glorious ascension, whereby 'dying, he destroyed our death, and, rising, He restored our life.'[1] For it was from the side of Christ as He slept the sleep of death upon the cross that there came forth 'the wondrous sacrament of the whole Church' "[2] (par. 5).

This leads to a view of Christ's saving work, and, more generally, to an understanding of the whole Christian faith, which puts the entire emphasis not on some abstract notions, but on the living unity of a saving event, which has to become ours, in the Church, through her sacramentality. But this view, so different from the impression conveyed by many handbooks of theology and different, too, from what remains a far too common way of preaching, becomes still more articulate in the next paragraph.

---

[1] Easter Preface of the Roman Missal.

[2] Prayer before the second lesson for Holy Saturday (as in the Roman missal before the abridgement of the Easter Vigil).

"Just as Christ was sent by the Father, so also He sent the apostles, filled with the Holy Spirit. This He did, not only that, by preaching the gospel to every creature, they might proclaim that the Son of God, by His death and resurrection, had freed us from the power of Satan and from death, and brought us into the kingdom of the Father; but also that they might achieve the work of salvation which they had proclaimed, by means of sacrifice and sacraments, around which the whole liturgical life revolves. . . ."

Therefore, the conclusion of that paragraph will be, "From that time onward, the Church has never failed to come together to celebrate the Paschal Mystery: reading those things 'which were in all the Scripture concerning Him' (Luke 24:27), celebrating the Eucharist in which 'the victory and triumph of His death are again made present,'[3] and at the same time giving thanks 'to God for His unspeakable gift' (II Cor. 9:15) in Christ Jesus, 'in praise of His glory' (Eph. 1:12), through the power of the Holy Spirit" (par. 6).

These admirable texts restore to us, in all its freshness, a view of Christianity possessed by the Fathers of the Church, both Greek and Latin, Eastern and Western. It means, once again, that faith is not just an intellectual assent to a series of dogmatic propositions, but the awakening consciousness of a divine and human history, which

---

[3] Council of Trent, Session XIII, Decree on the Holy Eucharist, c.5.

should become, and may actually become, our own history. It is the sacred history of salvation. As such, it has happened once and for all, reaching its summit in our Lord's life, and especially in His cross. However, everyone of us is directly concerned with it. This does not merely mean that the history of salvation is to have far-reaching consequences. It means rather that, from the beginning, we were—all mankind was—involved in it. And it means above all that we are now, in some mysterious but fully real way, to experience it as part of our own history. As the Council says, again in par. 6, quoting Saint Paul and emphasizing the full sense of what he says: ". . . By baptism men are plunged into the Paschal Mystery of Christ: they die with Him, are buried with Him;[4] they receive the Spirit of adoption as sons, 'in which we cry: Abba, Father' (Rom. 8:15), and they become true adorers whom the Father seeks"[5] (par. 6).

That view of the faith, which was that of the Fathers and which remains embodied in the traditional texts of Catholic liturgy, is not just a fanciful view of their own. It is not a merely rhetorical, more imaginative than theological, view, to be discarded or put aside as "vague," or "obsolete," terms persistently evoked against the

---

[4] See the first sentences of Rom. 6.
[5] Cf. John 4:23.

liturgical movement by those who, until quite recently, rejected it as cranky. It is, as the Council makes so clear, *the* view of the Church forever, precisely because it springs forth from the whole of Scripture. It is the view of the Word of God, as the Church has always understood it, and which she could not abandon without turning her back on her divine Master.

Here it must be admitted that the school of Maria Laach, while again bringing that vision into full light, perhaps sometimes unfortunately conveyed the impression that it was merely something out of the past, something from a religious culture which could not be revived. The attempt to explain the Christian mystery exclusively or mainly in the context of the pagan mysteries of the first centuries was more or less unfortunate, because it tended, contrary to the hopes of its own promoters (Dom Casel and his disciples) to obscure our appreciation of the creative originality, and therefore, everlasting validity, of that great vision of Christianity. However, the Council simply bypasses all the needless controversies which have arisen from that mistake, by leading us to the biblical sources and adhering to the basic biblical formulation of the mystery.

First of all, it introduces the Paschal mystery, not as the product of some special cultural milieu, but as the fullness of that revelation of God in His word, which is both word and action, revelation and event. "God who 'wills that all men be saved and come to the knowledge of the truth' (I Tim. 2:4), 'who in many and various ways spoke in times past to the fathers by the prophets' (Heb. 1:1), when the fullness of time had come sent His Son, the Word made flesh, anointed by the Holy Spirit, to preach the gospel to the poor, to heal the contrite of heart, to be a 'bodily and spiritual healer,'[6] the Mediator between God and man.[7] For His humanity, united with the person of the Word, was the instrument of our salvation. Therefore, in Christ 'the perfect achievement of our reconciliation came forth, and the fullness of divine worship was given to us.'[8] The wonderful works of God among the people of the Old Testament were the prelude to the work of Christ the Lord in redeeming mankind and giving perfect glory to God" (par. 5).

It is immediately after these words that the Council gives the definition of the Paschal Mystery quoted above. They, in truth, set this mystery in its proper perspective, the only one in which it can be rightly and fully understood. It is the perspective of the Word of God attaining its fullness from the Old through the New Testament. And this—we may state it now although

---

[6] St. Ignatius of Antioch, *To the Ephesians*, 7, 2.

[7] Cf. I Tim. 2:5.

[8] *Sacramentarium Veronense* (ed. Mohlberg), n. 1265; cf. also n. 1241, 1248.

later we shall have to develop it more fully—is the explanation of the insistence with which the Council enjoins a renewal in the knowledge of, and familiarity with, Scripture, as a necessary prerequisite for any liturgical renaissance.

What then, in Scripture, is the meaning of the "mystery," and what, in the same source, gives us the clue to that phrase, "Paschal mystery"?

In Scripture, first of all, a mystery (or rather, *the* mystery) is not just any truth which we are to receive without being able to fully explain, or even understand. Nor is it, as in some cults of later paganism, a sacred rite, to be kept out of reach, or even from the knowledge, of the profane multitudes, and jealously reserved to an esoteric coterie. It is the great secret of God's design for the salvation of the world. That secret could not be discovered even by the highest human wisdom. Indeed, it so much surpasses its capacity that, even once revealed, human wisdom cannot grasp it: the wise of this world are simply bewildered by its revelation. It seems like foolishness to them. And that is not so surprising, for neither men—not even the wisest among them— nor the angels themselves could achieve that knowledge without a special revelation of God, and the communication together of His own Spirit.

Therefore, from its first appearance in the first and second chapters of the first epistle of Saint

Paul to the Corinthians, this mystery is linked with the wisdom of God and its communication: the revelation of His word.

In the Old Testament, especially in the second chapter of Daniel, we find the word "mystery" used in the same connection already, with both wisdom and revelation. And there from the very beginning, it is a secret concerning human history, but one which God's intervention was to bring to fulfillment. In *Daniel*, God, who is the only real King of the world, and therefore the only really Wise One, is also the only one who knows the secret of what will happen in the fullness of time, since that depends wholly on His will. In Saint Paul, in the same way, only God possesses wisdom worthy of the name. That is to say, He alone knows the whole pattern of history, because it is wholly in His hands. It is dominated by a great design of His, in which every thing and every man, without reservation, must concur. And the final key of that heavenly design is the Cross of Christ.

In Christ alone, and chiefly in His passion as it leads to His resurrection, can be seen the wisdom of God coming to its final realization, and at the same time to its final disclosure. However, such a wisdom remains so far above any created understanding that it can be grasped only by faith, in the Spirit, that Spirit of which the risen Christ has become for us the only source.

In that light, the mystery is the great revelation of God's wisdom in Christ. It comes to us because in Christ the word of God to man reaches its ultimate fullness. That word, in Him as in the whole Bible which led to Him, is both revelation and fact. It is fully revealed to us in what Christ has said, but still more in what He has done among us, in what He is and in what He remains for us in His heavenly glory. Above all it is revealed in His Cross, in the light the Cross casts on all the sacred history which prepared us for it, in the light it casts on our own human history, even while it discloses to us something of the most hidden life of God: His fatherly love.

When the revelation of this mystery is given, then the whole of Scripture, the whole of sacred history, the whole of human history, become, in the light of God's love, wonderfully one. Conversely, confronted by the deepest experience of man's suffering and sin, and by man's unconquerable aspiration, we need the whole of Scripture in order to discover, under the inner illumination of the Spirit, what the Cross means for us and for the whole world.

And thus we pass from the mystery in general to the *Paschal* mystery. Why is that qualification applied to the mystery of the Cross? Not, indeed, just because the Cross happened on the day of the Paschal celebration, but because, in the Old Testament, that celebration of the Pasch was what, from the first, pointed to the Cross, and was, at the last, that which would uncover the meaning of it. Saint Paul himself, as well as the whole primitive Church, understood and expounded the Cross as the true Pasch, as that mystery which had from the first been lying under what the Pasch prepared, sketched, promised to the faithful people of God: "Christ, our Passover, has been immolated! . . ." (I Cor. 5:7).

Primitively, the Pasch had been just one of those spring festivals which were also to remain at the core of the pagan mysteries of Hellenism. It was the festival of life reappearing on the surface of the earth after the apparent death of winter. But, at a decisive turn in the history of Israel, it had taken on a new meaning. Henceforth, for the Israelites, it would no longer be a festival of creation, connected with the powers of nature. It would become and would remain forever the festival of redemption, connected with a single event: a single intervention of God in the history of mankind. It would therefore be a memorial: the memorial of the salvific intervention through which God had made something new forever in that history. It would be the memorial of the great act through which a People of God, a People known to God and knowing Him, would have been disengaged from the mass of men, lost in indifference and sin.

"Passover," in the Bible, is explained first of

all by the fact that God, "visiting" Egypt on the night when the Paschal meal was eaten by the Hebrews, "passed over" the Hebrew houses. That is to say, He spared those who were feasting in the expectation of His salvation, while He chastised those who despised these others and their faith in Him. In every house of Egypt where the feast had not been observed, there was to be death on the morrow. Only those houses of the faithful Israelites, where the blood of the Lamb could be seen on the lintel of the door, were spared.

But even in the Old Testament, combined with that first interpretation we find the idea that God, passing through Egypt, and "passing over" Israel, has caused Israel, together with Himself, to pass from Egypt to the promised land. They will pass through the Red Sea, through the desert, later through the Jordan, and thus from the land of bondage to the land of freedom, from exile to home. And this, in itself, was much more than a merely material deliverance. It was a complete renewal (if not the total creation) of the filial consciousness of Israel towards its God. It was, therefore, a passage from darkness to light, from death to life. It was redemption, in the basic meaning of the word: the ransom paid for the slave, which makes of him a man at last, and here an adopted son of Him who has paid it for him.

Thus, the death of Christ on the Cross, on the

eve of the Pasch, at the very time when the Paschal lamb had to be immolated, will be interpreted as the true Pasch: that in which all the figures and the explicit or implicit promises connected with the old Pasch become a lasting and perfect reality. It is, first of all, the intervention of God in our history which has manifested to the full His mercy, His unutterable love to us, while it has condemned and deprived our spiritual foes of all their power over us. Sin and death itself, its most hideous and revealing consequence, have been overcome. The world, which was enticing us to sin, our own flesh, whose rebellious instincts brought us to death, and in them the devil, who was using both to turn us from our Creator, are now impotent to separate us from that great love He has manifested to us in His Son, crucified for our sins in our flesh. Even His own Law is not able to frighten or crush us any more: its condemnation of us has been nailed to the Cross, while on it we have been reconciled with God, in the body of His Son.

Therefore, the mystery of the Cross is also that Pasch by which we pass from the power of darkness to the Kingdom of Light, the Kingdom of that love of the Father that the Son has made known to us. Through the death of Christ, in it, we are brought from death to life, from the death of this world to the resurrection of the world to come. From the flesh, we pass with the risen

Christ to the Spirit. From the law of our condemnation, we obtain access to the grace of infinite love. The bondage in which we were kept by the devil has been replaced for us by the freedom of the children of God. In that freedom all creation can see a token, and some earnest, of His glory, soon to be revealed throughout a creation that has been brought back to His eternal design.

Moreover, in the Old Testament the Pasch was annually renewed as a standing memorial to God's saving action, not merely in the sense that this unique event was commemorated year after year. As the Protestant exegete Jeremias has made perfectly clear, "Memorial," in the language of the Bible as in the Jewish liturgy, meant far more. To say that the Pasch was the memorial of the Exodus meant that, in it, the Jews believed they were made partakers of the great event itself. As the Haggada, the explanation of the Pasch still recited in Jewish families at the Easter meal, has it: "*We, today*, are saved from the Egyptians. . . . *We, today*, are going through the Red Sea. . . . *We, today*, are entering our inheritance. . . ." In the same way, even while the Cross was being revealed to the disciples at the Lord's Supper as the everlasting Pasch, for the redemption of all mankind, every Eucharist of the Christians was to be made the memorial of the Cross. If, according to Saint Paul, "every time we eat of this Bread and we drink from this Cup, we announce the death of the Lord, until He comes," it is not just as a reminder of something past. It is because through the Eucharist, in our common participation in the body and the blood of our crucified Lord, we become partakers of His Cross. This, properly, is the last word on the Paschal mystery, as embodied in the Liturgy. As the Council tells us, in the Christian celebration, not only is the mystery of Christ proclaimed by the apostolic ministry of the Church, but the work of salvation is accomplished as well: *opus redemptionis exercetur*. That formula of the Leonine sacramentary —still used in our missal, and so pregnant with meaning—was always quoted by Dom Casel as lifting the veil on the mysterious reality of the whole sacramental order. And, as it can be seen in the central text of the constitution quoted above, the Council has also found in it the best possible expression of the active presence of the Paschal mystery in the Liturgy. As a commentary on it, the Council immediately quotes Saint Paul on baptism and eucharist. "Thus by baptism men are plunged into the paschal mystery of Christ: they die with Him, are buried with Him, and rise with Him. . . . In like manner, as often as they eat the Supper of the Lord, they proclaim the death of the Lord until He comes. . ." (par. 6).

Therefore, just as to proclaim God's word, in the biblical fullness of the phrase, is to lead to its accomplishment, through its own virtue, that memorial of Christ's mystery which is the core of the Christian celebration is not opposed to its actual reality. It is rather the principle of it. In that memorial, which Christ the saving Word Himself gives, He testifies that He is still present with us, to make His great work for us fully our own. And, in our turn, insofar as we who are faithful to this intention and obedient to His command present His memorial to the Father, we pledge ourselves to live henceforth not to ourselves, but in His only Son, in the power of His cross and His resurrection, through the Spirit, by whom we cry: "Abba! Father!" The memorial of the Paschal mystery, therefore—in the Mass first of all, but through the whole sacramental celebration—is both that great sacrament of the Church through which all grace comes to us from the Father from above, and the perfect Sacrifice of the Whole Christ, through which the Body together with its divine Head becomes acceptable, before the Father. . . .

When we consider—in the very first words of the first text which it has canonized—that presentation of Catholic truth to which the Council has returned us, can we fail to perceive the wonderful unity of the vision thus opened to our faith? Don't we realize, at the same time, how such a vision makes the truth alive, for men of today as of all times? We should rather say: it just evokes from us that permanent freshness, that vibrant appeal which is inherent in divine truth as we find it in the word of God itself. It was the great and lasting merit of the Fathers of the Church to have kept the divine truth in this, its primitive, presentation. And it is the permanent privilege of the liturgy to maintain it for us, ever so fresh, ever so full of life, ever so one, of the unity of life. For it is not just one possible explanation of the liturgy. It is the explanation that the liturgy never ceases to give us of itself, if only we pay attention to what it tells us, and how it tells it.

However, how far have we strayed from such an ideal, and at the same time so real, presentation of the truth? Not only in the abstract theology of most of our modern textbooks, but even in our catechetical teaching, in our daily preaching—what remains of it? Too often, we have substituted for it a dry collection of correct but uninspiring formulae, which stink up the atmosphere of the classroom and retain very little of the fragrance of God's own words. If we are ever to remake the liturgy into a living and appealing reality, we must first of all think and speak in that way. The Council insists on the necessity, for the clergy first of all, not only to have a canonical or rubrical knowledge of the liturgy, but to understand it, to be made fully aware of its wealth of teaching and of inspiration, so that they may become able to lead their people to "a full, active

and conscious participation." Without that pre-
liminary, all efforts toward a restoration of the
liturgy will fall flat. How many priests even now
complain that the reform of Holy Week, especially the restoration of the Easter vigil, has had
little or no practical effect? How could it have
been otherwise if the Christian people have not
been made aware of the true significance of those
most sacred celebrations of the Church? And how
could they be made aware so long as their clergy
are so insensitive, and, therefore, so little influenced, either in their spiritual practice or in their
teaching by the spirit of the liturgy itself? Thus,
much more than on any reform of the rites—however important that may be—the future of the
whole liturgical movement and the renovation of
the entire life of the Church will depend, first of
all, on the full and practical understanding that
the clergy will acquire of that basic teaching of
the Conciliar constitution concerning the Paschal
mystery.

II

THE MYSTERY OF WORSHIP

WE CAN ACCURATELY SAY THAT THE CONCILIAR CONSTI-
tution has consecrated the teaching of the school
of Maria Laach, first of all in the description of
Christianity as being the Paschal mystery of
Christ. But we can go even further and also state
that the Constitution has made it clear that Dom
Casel and his disciples were correct when they
insisted that this mystery is the mystery of worship, that is, that mystery, the reality of which
lies behind the liturgy. That, probably, was the
point which seemed most difficult to accept for
many theologians today. In the objections raised
against it, we can detect the rationalism of many
who call themselves Thomists, but who owe
much more to the "clear and distinct ideas" dear
to Descartes than to the profound thinker for
whom analogy, and not univocity, of being was
the only feasible basis of theology.

That profound idea of the Mystery ever present behind the sacred rites, which gives to them

their spiritual content, seemed mere misty thinking to its opponents. How, they said, could an
event of the past ever be reiterated, so as to become, in any intelligible sense, a reality of today?
Wiser on this point than in some of his historical
explanations of the mystery, wherein he made a
dubious appeal to the pagan mysteries, Dom
Casel constantly refrained from attempting to
explain the fact. Quite correctly he simply insisted that neither the liturgical texts themselves,
nor the commentaries on them produced by the
Fathers, could be understood if the fact was not
admitted; or rather, if it was not admitted that it
was a fact for them. Less happy, perhaps, were
certain attempts at a philosophical explanation,
like that suggested by Söhngen, that a Platonic,
rather than Aristotelian, approach could render
more palatable the idea of present participation
in a past event. Casel felt that it was not a matter
of philosophy, and that, posed in such an abstract
and general way, the question was probably not
susceptible of any satisfactory answer. It was
rather a purely theological question: how do the
actions of God in Christ, even when happening
at some precise epoch, for once and for all, in-
volve all of us and reach all of us through every
age? Therefore, he would more readily accept
Abbot Vonier's fine analysis of the sacramental
action and presence, based on St. Thomas. According to that view, the sacramental action is

not just a new action, but a mysterious extension
to us, through the ritual, of an action of Christ
the Head, accomplished once and for all time, but
from the first concerning the whole mystical body
and now at last extending to it. It is the same line
of thought that Father Schillebeeckx would later
develop so forcefully.

However, as might be expected, the Council
has not entered into such technical discussions,
however interesting they may be. But it has made
its own the essential points: by the sacramental
celebration "men are plunged into the Paschal
mystery of Christ," and this happens because,
especially in the eucharistic celebrations, "the victory and triumph of His death are again made
present" (par. 6). This last quotation of the Council of Trent is here fully expressive: *mortis ejus
victoria et triumphus repraesentatur*, both because it was again and again quoted by Casel,
even though his adversaries tried to prove it
did not mean as much as he said, and because
it is clear that it means just as much for the
Council.

Rather, then, than enter into any analysis of
the way in which the action of Christ becomes our
own in the liturgy, the Council insists on the fact
that He is always present in the Church, especially in her liturgical actions. And it seems that,
for the Council, it is the multiform aspects of
that presence which in the twilight of faith can

best help us see how the mystery of Christ is to become—as we see it in Saint Paul's captivity epistles—"Christ in us, the hope of our glory" (Col. 1:27).

After it has just mentioned the perpetual celebration of the Paschal mystery in the liturgy of the Church, the Council adds these most significant words:

"To accomplish so great a work, Christ is always present in His Church, especially in her liturgical celebrations. He is present in the sacrifice of the Mass, both in the person of the minister, 'the same now offering, through the ministry of priests, who formerly offered Himself on the cross,'[9] and especially under the eucharistic species. By His power, He is present in the sacraments, so that when a man baptizes it is really Christ Himself who baptizes. He is present in His word, since it is He Himself who speaks when the Holy Scriptures are read in the Church. He is present, lastly, when the Church prays and sings, for He promised: 'Where two or three are gathered together in my name, there I am in the midst of them' (Matt. 18:20).

"Christ, indeed, always associates the Church with Himself in this great work wherein God is perfectly glorified and men are sanctified. The Church is His beloved Bride who calls to her Lord,

---

[9] Council of Trent, Session XXII, Decree on the Holy Sacrifice of the Mass, c.2.

and through Him offers worship to the eternal Father" (par. 7).

I think that in these few lines we have a great wealth and depth of doctrine. Let us try only to make it as explicit as possible, while adding as little as possible of our own thoughts to it. It is so full in itself that it is best to let it speak for itself. The Council mentions first the presence of Christ in the priest, seen above all as the minister of the Eucharist. This leads us to a consideration of the apostolic ministry as the principle of the entire life of the Church. What happens in the Church happens because Christ has sent men—the Apostles—in whom He is present in some way, just as God was present in Christ whom He sent. Let us turn again to the first words of par. 6 (commented on above): "Just as Christ was sent by the Father, so also He sent the apostles filled with the Holy Spirit." This, you remember, was given as the basis for both the preaching of the gospels and the celebration of the sacraments, above all of the Eucharist. What does it mean? It means that the meaning of the Church itself is to extend, as it were, the presence, the active presence, of Christ to us. This is possible because Christ has manifested His will to be with us, in a mysterious way, through the ministry of the Apostles (and the bishops, in so far as they are the successors of the Apostles, and finally of every priest, as a co-operator of his bishop). Thus, when Christ's word is brought to us, it is not only His word materially which is echoed, but He Himself indeed who continues to speak it to us. In the same way, in the sacramental action, His action, the decisive action of His earthly life: the Paschal mystery, is extended to us by Him, or, if we prefer it, we are taken into it.

This is the fundamental presence of Christ in and with His Church. And it is the reason why the Church is built on the foundation of the Apostles (which means the foundation they are, *qua* apostles).

However, this is only a means to an end. As Saint Thomas explains it fully, just as baptism is the basis of every individual Christian life, the sacrament of order, in so far as it extends the primitive apostolate through the centuries, is the basis of the life of the whole Church. But the Church, he continues, is built on this basis mainly by the eucharistic celebration. The ministerial priesthood, in prolonging unto us the apostolic ministry, is exercised *par excellence* in the mass. We shall see later how this is to be understood in a fullness of meaning too often neglected by commentators. It means far more than the power to consecrate. However, now, to follow the thought of the Council which leads us immediately from the presence of Christ in the ministerial priesthood to His presence in the eucharistic species, we will do well to concentrate our thought on the

Thomistic definition of that priesthood: a power over the physical body of Christ for the development of His mystical body. Here again, what does that mean? It means that through the Eucharistic celebration the Body of Christ, that body which was slain for our redemption and which rose again for our justification, is now made present. And it is made present as our food. That is to say, so that we may become one with it, and one in it. As Saint Paul says: "Is not the bread that we break the communion to the body of Christ? . . . Now therefore, since there is one bread, as many as we are, we are one body, all who have partaken of that one bread" (I Cor. 10:16-17). To come back to Saint Thomas: we have the bread as a mere sign (*sacramentum tantum*); and that sign is the sign of a reality, which is there, but only, in its turn, as another sign leading further (*res et sacramentum*): he means that body of Christ which was crucified and is now glorified in heaven; and finally the ultimate reality to which it leads us (through our communion to it and in it) is that perfect unity of the mystical body of Christ, the Church, which will be reached fully only in heaven (*res tantum*).

In other words, the announcement of the gospel of the Cross by the apostolic ministry, the eucharistic celebration in which what has been announced is communicated to us—all this leads finally to our becoming the body (mystical) of

Christ through our participation in His body (physical), since in it He Himself has gone through death to eternal life.

In other sacraments besides the eucharist, which the Council considers after that, Christ, again as in the apostolic ministry, is there by His power (*virtute sua*). We can understand that in them (and first of all in baptism) He does not so much make present the Mystery of His Cross, since that is achieved in a unique way in the eucharist, but rather "plunges us into it" (*mysterio inseruntur*). In other words, in the other sacraments we are, as it were, adapted to Christ and to the different aspects of His mystery, so that in the Eucharist we may really partake of it and not just be present in the way the witnesses of His passion were present at the foot of the cross: seeing it, touching it perhaps, but unable to take part in it.

All this together, under the visible tokens of grace that Christ Himself has given us, is accomplished "through the power of the Spirit" (par. 6), which He has given to His Church with these signs, and without which they would be only mere show. The sacramental signs, finally, are nothing else than an extension to us by Christ Himself, the word made flesh, of that great and primordial sacrament which is Himself, and through which the Spirit of God is given to us.

If, without trying to go beyond the teaching of

the Council, we try only to assemble the complementary aspects of the Mystery in the same perspective in which they are presented in the words of the Council, we can perhaps see in the best possible light how the mystery is ever present at the heart of the worship of the Church.

It is present because Christ, once crucified and forever sitting in the glory of the Father, is still present with His Church. However, it is not present with us now as it was present on Calvary: it is not present before our eyes but as an object of our faith, as a pattern our lives are now to reproduce, so as not to be any longer merely our life, but Christ living in us. And that, finally, is made possible through the Spirit of God, of which the risen Christ has become for us the everlasting source—through His acceptance of the passion— and which He gives us here and now in the way of a "memorial" of the passion. Thus only we may partake of the mystery, and through it attain to that fullness of life, as a full and perfect body, at which our Head, following that way, that Pasch, that *"transitus,"* has arrived and in which He remains forever.

At this point in the liturgy, therefore, we are led to see the relation of Christ to us along the lines of the epistle to the Hebrews. In that epistle, Christ is described as our High Priest, but this title is further explained as meaning that He is our forerunner: He who, through the sacrifice of

His blood, has obtained access for us all to the
immediate presence of the Father. Such a view
will soon enable us to discover a deeper meaning
in that qualification of the mystery called the
mystery of worship. However, let us first return
to the last two points in the Council's enumera-
tion of the different and complementary ways of
the Presence of Christ with His Church, in worship. "He is present in His word, since it is He
Himself who speaks when the Holy Scriptures
are read in the Church. He is present, lastly, when
the Church prays and sings, for He promised:
'Where two or three are gathered together in my
name, there I am in the midst of them'" (Matt.
18:20) (par. 7).

How are we to understand this last paragraph?
Are we here to discover, to complete, two last
modes of Christ's presence in His Church, to be
added to those we have studied up to now? I do
not believe the text is to be interpreted in that
way. Rather, I believe, the presence of Christ,
both in the word spoken *to the Church*, and in
the answer, the response evoked by it *in the
Church*, is to be seen as the alpha and the omega
of the sacramental presence under its complementary aspects. In Christianity, the whole encounter of man with God, or rather of God with
man, is perpetuated in the liturgy. There, as ever,
that encounter begins with God speaking to man,
intervening in man's life through His word. The

first manifestation of God's Word is always in human words, but those words, on God's own lips, soon lead to deed: to a divine action, which is not, however, intended to suppress but to restore man's action. The hand of God is to touch us, to seize upon us, so that we may do with Him what we could not do without Him. However, the hand of God, like His voice, touches us only in the God-made-man. Therefore, it will not absorb our freedom under its almighty power, but make it more fruitful. The word of God is not spoken to us for any other purpose than to evoke our response: a response of our whole being. That response will be sacrificial, just like the Word spoken to us. But also, just like the sacrifice of the Word, it will lead us only to the fullness, the plenitude of life. And the response, like the word, must culminate in deed, in action. But being the response of intelligent and free beings, it must, like the divine Word itself, begin with human words. These are the words of prayer, and especially of praise, because the first prayer in answer to the divine Word must always be praise.

And in the prayer of man, above all in the perfect prayer of praise, the Eucharist, the God-made-man is to be present as He was first present in the Word spoken to us. It may even be said that He made Himself present in our flesh, under our human words as under our human action, only to be finally present *in us*: in our own words,

and in the whole life they imply. That last presence, through the Spirit of God, the Spirit of the
Lord who was crucified but who, risen again, is
now forever at the right of the Father, that presence which gives us a new life, fully human but
fully divine, is the purpose of the whole sacramental presence of Christ with us. By it, the Spirit
and the Bride cry together: "Come, O Lord, come
quickly!" For the Spirit in us makes us wait for
that last coming of the Lord, in glory, for which
His hidden coming in the Word and the sacraments prepares us: that last coming in which He
will take us with Him forever, and bring us, together with Himself, into the immediate presence
of the Father.

This leads us to a deeper apprehension of the
mystery of worship. It is not only the mystery
underlying the worship of the Church, but the
mystery which enables us to worship the Father
"in Spirit and in truth." As the Council says:
through our participation in the Mystery, we
"become true adorers whom the Father seeks"
(par. 6).

More generally, throughout the Conciliar Constitution it is striking to notice that every mention of the sanctifying effect of the liturgy on
those who take part in it is immediately complemented by a mention of the glorification of God
thus achieved. That the Council does not simply
mean that both things go together, but rather

that the sanctification of man consists of his being enabled to glorify God, is made clear, however, by a text like this:

"Christ indeed always associates the Church with Himself in the great work wherein God is perfectly glorified and men are sanctified. The Church is His beloved Bride who calls to her Lord, and through Him offers worship to the eternal Father.

"Rightly, then, the liturgy is considered as an exercise of the priestly office of Jesus Christ in which the sanctification of man is signified by signs perceptible to the senses, and is effected in a way which corresponds with each of these signs, so that the whole public worship is performed by the mystical body of Jesus Christ, that is, by the head and His members. From this it follows that every liturgical celebration, because it is an action of Christ the priest, and of His body which is the Church, is a sacred action surpassing all others; no other action of the Church can equal its efficacy by the same title and to the same degree" (par. 7).

In the preceding points we met again and again with some of the foremost teachings of Dom Casel, often in his own words. Here we are brought back, in the same way, to the fundamental doctrine of Dom Lambert Beauduin, the great initiator of all the liturgical movements of the twentieth century, in the movement he began in Belgium before the First World War. The liturgy is the exercise of the priestly function of Christ, associating the Church to Himself in it. And, by being that, it makes clear that the sanctification of man finds its supreme goal in making of man a true worshiper, or adorer, of the Father. Sanctification, seen in that light, is a movement upward, through which man is reoriented, no longer absorbed in himself or in the world, but referring both himself and the whole world to God alone. Praise, exultant glorification of God, self-surrender and self-dedication, not only to His will but to His sole glory, appear as the supreme end of all human activity. Of course, as Saint Irenaeus said, God achieves His glory in making man fully alive: *Gloria Dei, vivens homo!* But that has no meaning if we do not first understand that for man, made of mind and heart, the true life is to know God and to love Him. This is what will be our eternal life. And we are prepared for it, here on earth, in the measure in which we are enabled, even now, to inaugurate that life which we may well call a eucharistic life: a life of contemplation and adoration of God. This is the ultimate meaning of the liturgy and of the whole of Christianity. Of course, as we shall see, the liturgy has much to teach us. But, in the final analysis, it is to teach us the life of adoration. The liturgy is again to transform our being, to restore it, to elevate it: this is what we mean by sancti-

fication. But sanctification itself is nothing if it is
not a consecration of our whole life to the glorification of God by all the powers of our minds
and hearts, taking into our upsurge toward God
our bodies, our activities, corporal as well as
spiritual: finally, all human life, individual as
well as social.

Here is the meaning of that royal priesthood,
described by the first epistle of Saint Peter. In it,
the laity as well as the clergy—the whole people
of God—are to become, in the unity of the mystical body, one cosmic priest, making of the whole
universe a single offering to the heavenly Father.
It is for that that in the liturgy Christ, as the High
Priest of the Father, unites His Bride the Church
to His priestly function. This is the view of His
cross, leading to His resurrection and ascension,
which is given us by the epistle to the Hebrews.
And its normal consequence is the description of
the Church, found in the same epistle, as the
"panegyry," that is, the festive assembly in which
God is to be praised forever. Hence the great
visions of the apocalypse: of the elect, the faithful witnesses of the Lamb, being united with the
Lamb in the immediate presence of God, to take
their part in the everlasting Sanctus of the an-
gelic creation.

This is exactly what the Conciliar Constitution
evokes in the paragraph that follows the last
quoted:

"In the earthly liturgy we take part in a fore-
taste of the heavenly liturgy which is celebrated
in the holy city of Jerusalem towards which we
journey as pilgrims, where Christ is sitting at the
right hand of God, a minister of the holies and
of the true tabernacle;[10] we sing a hymn to the
Lord's glory with all the warriors of the heavenly
army; venerating the memory of the saints, we
hope for some part and fellowship with them; we
eagerly await the Savior, our Lord Jesus Christ,
until He, our life, shall appear and we too will
appear with Him in glory"[11] (par. 8).

Let us not consider that beautiful text merely
as a burst of enthusiasm on the part of the Fathers
of the Council, or still less as an ornamental flash
of rhetoric. If we do not take it seriously, we
shall never get at the essentials of the liturgy. As
we shall see in greater detail, the liturgy will never
be properly understood by us as long as we
merely try to use it, to turn it even to our best
pastoral or pedagogical preoccupations. Of
course, it has an immense pastoral effect, as a
most wonderful pedagogy. But the liturgical
pedagogy, we must not tire of repeating, is a
pedagogy *of worship*. Its pastoral aim, therefore,
can be none other than that of making the whole
Christian flock—to borrow a most felicitous

---

[10] Cf. Apoc. 21:2; Col. 3:1; Heb. 8:2.
[11] Cf. Phil. 3:20; Col. 3:4.

phrase from Dom Guéranger—"the society of the divine praise."

This basic approach to the liturgy will be rediscovered only if we rediscover the full importance of the divine office, as first of all a great prayer of praise. Of course, it centers on the mass, on the eucharistic sacrifice; but we will never properly understand what the Christian sacrifice is itself if we do not see it primarily in the light of the prayer in which it is offered. If this prayer is called eucharist, or thanksgiving, it is not just in the impoverished sense of a mere expression of gratitude for the benefit of God's grace. It is in the primitive sense of full praise of all the *magnalia Dei*, the great works of God, centering and attaining their perfection in that single offering of our divine Head. With Him and in Him the whole people of God shall appear before the face of God saying, or rather singing, with all that is in man, purified and elevated by the Holy Spirit: "Our Father, who art in heaven, hallowed be Thy Name!"

III

THE MYSTERY OF
THE CHURCH

IN WHAT WE HAVE ALREADY SAID, THE INTIMATE CON-
nection between the mystery and the Church
must have become manifest. It is made so clear,
indeed, according to the Council's teaching, that
the Mystery of worship can be called, with equal
accuracy, the Mystery of the Church. Here again
we mean first the Mystery which is to be found
in the Church, but only to be later discerned as
the Mystery of the Church herself: the Mystery
of her life, of her progressive building in history.

If the mystery is what we have described, it
may be readily understood that the liturgy in
which it is embodied must be considered as the
great treasure of the Church, and therefore the
object *par excellence* of the responsibility for
those who are in authority in the Church. For it
is not a treasure that the Church could enjoy
freely as its possession. It is a treasure committed
to her care, to her ministry, for the whole world
of men. She is not the master of this treasure, free

to use or abuse, but the warden. The liturgy, in which the word of God is announced, the sacraments celebrated, and man therefore introduced to the participation of the Paschal Mystery and the worship "in Spirit and in truth" of the Father, constitutes the main mission of the apostolic ministry. The Apostles, and after them the bishops as their successors, have been made responsible for it. Therefore, no authority other than theirs can order the celebration of the liturgy. Even the most zealous or the most learned priests are not entitled to change or alter substantially anything in it. The insistence of the Council on this point must be underlined. "Regulation of the sacred liturgy depends solely on the authority of the Church, that is, on the apostolic See, and, as laws may determine, on the bishop.

"In virtue of power conceded by the law, the regulation of the liturgy within certain defined limits belongs also to various kinds of competent territorial bodies of bishops, legitimately established.

"Therefore, no other person, even if he be a priest, may add, remove, or change anything in the liturgy on his own authority.

"That sound traditions may be retained, and yet that the way may remain open to legitimate progress, a careful investigation must always be made into each part of the liturgy which is to be revised. This investigation should be theological,

historical and pastoral. Also, the general laws
governing the structure and meaning of the liturgy must be studied in conjunction with the
experience derived from recent liturgical reforms
and from the indults conceded to various places.
Finally, there must be no innovations unless the
good of the Church genuinely and certainly requires them; and care must be taken that any new
forms adopted should in some way grow organically from forms already existing.

"As far as possible, notable differences between the rites used in adjacent regions must be
carefully avoided" (par. 22-23).

Such insistence on the exclusive right of the
episcopal body, always in conjunction with the
Roman See, does not mean that this right is an
arbitrary power. It is not to be understood, as has
been declared too often, that the liturgy is something external, decorative, a mere matter of cere-
monial, and hence authority can direct it without
paying regard to any superior law or principle.
To believe this would be to forget, first, that in the
liturgy we have a most sacred expression and realization of the divine truth, and then, that the
apostolic authority which the bishops exercise is
not an authority which enables them to substantially modify or dispense with anything that has
been transmitted as coming from the Twelve
Apostles. To interpret the apostolic authority of
the bishops in that way would be to confirm all

the worst prejudices of the Protestants against the Catholic doctrine of apostolic succession. If such, indeed, could be the meaning of this doctrine, then the Protestant would be fully justified in denouncing and impugning it as a radical corruption of the Gospel. However, the proper meaning is just the opposite: the apostolic authority of the bishops has been given them, not to destroy, not to alter in any way what has been done by the Apostles once and for all, but to keep it, and to keep it alive. In other words, they only have authority to alter those things which, through a secular evolution, no longer express and achieve what the Apostles intended. They can modify the liturgy only to maintain its living authenticity under altered circumstances. And that is why most of the modifications introduced by episcopal authority are only a return to more ancient practices that have been obliterated by routine, negligence or ignorance, while the few real innovations contemplated will always tend only to provide a substantial (and not merely material) equivalent of what the Apostles did, in circumstances wherein the material means the Apostles employed could no longer be understood according to the meaning they attached to them.

This is why the action of the bishops in the domain of reform or adaptation is described by the Council not as a reversal of, but as a deeper fidelity to, tradition. Tradition is not opposed to

progress, but is the living principle of a development faithful to the seed, however altered may
be the soil where it has to rise, flower and fruc-
tify. And the Council is careful to make it perfectly clear, in opposition to all false reforms—
which start only from abstract ideas—that tradition cannot be maintained either by unprece-
dented innovations or by artificial archaisms.
All healthy progress, as well as all true reforma-
tions, can only be effected by an organic process.
One can neither add wholly foreign elements to
the liturgy from the outside, nor make it regress
to some idealized vision of the past. One can, and
sometimes should, either prune or enrich the liturgy, but he should always keep in touch with the
living organism which has been transmitted to us
by our forefathers, and he should always respect
the laws of its structure and of its growth. No
innovation, therefore, can be accepted simply for
the purpose of doing something new, and no restoration can be the product of a yen for romantic
escape into a dead past. The continuity, the
homogeneity of tradition in this case must be
retained by authority as the *sine qua non* condi-
tion for the perpetuated life of a reality which is
not merely immensely sacred but even the very
life of the mystical body.

It is finally precisely because the liturgy is the
life of the body of Christ on earth that the bishops
are the only ones who have authority to intervene

here, for they are the ones to whose sole care that life has been committed.

To understand this fully, we must pass on to what the Council says concerning the unique relation of the bishop to the Church, as manifested in the liturgical celebration itself.

"The bishop is to be considered as the high priest of his flock, from whom the life in Christ of his faithful is in some way derived and dependent.

"Therefore, all should hold in great esteem the liturgical life of the diocese centered around the bishop, especially in his cathedral church; they must be convinced that the pre-eminent manifestation of the Church consists in the full active participation of all God's holy people in these liturgical celebrations, especially in the same eucharist, in a single prayer, at one altar, at which presides the bishop surrounded by his college of priests and by his ministers" (par. 41).[12]

Here we have a most important teaching, too often lost sight of, concerning first the bishop, and next the eucharist, both in connection with the Church.

The authority of the bishops, either individually or seen as a body, is not to be considered as the authority of a big and complex administrative

---

[12] Cf. St. Ignatius of Antioch, *To the Smyrnians*, 8; *To the Magnesians*, 7; *To the Philadelphians*, 4.

system organized around the Roman See, even as the Church itself is not to be understood primarily in terms of a universal power, tending to bring all men to its subjection. For the bishop, whether it be the pope himself or the bishop of the smallest diocese, is not primarily an administrator: he is a priest, and, more precisely a pastor. This means that his function is not related to an inhuman, anonymous bureaucracy, but to a group of human beings living together, meeting in true community, the links of which are both fully human and most sacred: "a same eucharist, a single prayer, at one altar." And this again means that the visibility of the Church, that in which her true nature is manifested to the world, is not primarily in any world organization, but in the gathering together of every man with his neighbors (in the Gospel's sense of the word) in and through the eucharistic celebration. As has been aptly said, the eucharist is the fundamental epiphany of the Church. And therefore, it is first of all in his celebration of the eucharist, with all its implications, that the bishop himself manifests the true nature of his power, as a successor of the Apostles. For it is there that he continues their work of building the Church as the mystical body of Christ: by announcing the Paschal Mystery of Christ and causing men to take part in that mystery, by their common participation being made one in His body, once dead and forever risen again.

When all that has been said, we can understand why the last two popes have been so careful to preach and celebrate the eucharist in the middle of their own local church. For no bishop can be seen acting as a bishop—and least of all he who is to preside over universal charity (as Saint Ignatius said, speaking of the Roman Church)— who is not seen in the middle of his flock, giving them nourishment both from the Word and from the flesh of Christ and thus providing for their common prayer as well as for their universal charity.

At the same time this helps us understand how the liturgical mystery is not only a mystery committed to the Church *for* the world, but *this* mystery precisely, through which the Church is to be built *out of* the world. For the Church is not built by administration or legislation, however indispensable these things may be. The Church is built where two or three are gathered together in the name of Christ, and where the apostolic ministry gathers them, indeed, in the full reality of this name, by announcing the gospel to them and breaking for them the bread of life.

This is supremely essential to the life of the Church, as the Council explains it in the following words:

". . . Because it is impossible for the bishop always and everywhere to preside over the whole flock in his Church, he cannot do other than establish lesser groupings of the faithful. Among these the parishes, set up locally under a pastor who takes the place of the bishop, are the most important: for in some manner they represent the visible Church constituted throughout the world" (par. 42).

Nothing could be more decisive in making us realize that the Church is, first of all, the community built into one body by the actual celebration of the Eucharist. In that sense, the liturgical mystery is, indeed, finally the mystery of the Church herself, coming to life and manifesting herself in the liturgical celebration.

Of course, because every parish celebrates its own eucharist in communion with its bishop (whose local co-operator is the pastor), and because every bishop is in communion with all other Catholic bishops around the Roman See, the Church, in every local celebration of the mass, extends invisibly to the confines of the world. But the Church is not only "represented," but represented in its actual constitution first of all by the common celebration of the eucharist. It is in it and through it that men become true and living members of a single body, that is Christ's own body, and the highest order of the ministry in the Church is ordained primarily to promote and consecrate this sacred gathering, focus of the whole liturgy as well as of the whole Christian life.

Hence ensues the importance, emphasized by the Council, of the liturgical celebration, and above all of the celebration of the mass, which appears—as it is—as a fully public and common action, in which all who are gathered become one in Christ.

"Liturgical services are not private functions, but are celebrations of the Church, the 'sacrament of unity,' namely, the holy people united and ordered under their bishops.[13] Therefore, liturgical services pertain to the whole body of the Church; they manifest it and have effects upon it; but they concern the individual members of the Church in different ways, according to their differing rank, office and actual participation. It is to be stressed that whenever rites, according to their specific nature, make provision for communal celebration involving the presence and active participation of the faithful, this way of celebrating them is to be preferred, wherever possible, to a celebration that is individual and quasi-private.

"This applies with especial force to the celebration of mass and the administration of the sacraments, it being understood that every mass has of itself a public and social nature" (par. 26-27). Here again, the doctrine expressed by the Council is to be seen in its fullness. The liturgy, and above

---

[13] St. Cyprian, *On the Unity of the Catholic Church*, 7; cf. Letter 66, n. 8, 3.

all, the mass, is the manifestation and actual realization of this "Sacrament of unity" which is the
Church herself. Therefore, to minimize in practice
its public and communal character is to run counter to its aim and its very essence. Here the Council exposes for once and for all the incredible
fallacy of the stand sometimes taken by some
theologians whose abstract legalism went to the
most extreme forms of nominalism. In that
way it has been said that since every mass is,
in itself and by itself, a public function, even if
there is nobody with the priest (although this, in
fact, is strictly forbidden by the rubrics and canon
law, which have always made compulsory the
attendance at least of one faithful, the server or
somebody answering), then it is quite useless
either to promote attendance or to encourage the
actual participation of those who may be there.
Such an incredible piece of sophistry is reduced
ad absurdum by the teaching of the Council. The
truth, of course, is the exact opposite. By the
very fact that there can be no mass that is not
public in principle (i.e., that does not tend to
gather into one the scattered children of God),
every mass, whenever and to whatever extent
possible, is to be celebrated in the most public
way, that is, with the proper attendance and participation of the people.

More especially, it is directly opposed to the
very essence of the mass that more than one be

offered in the same place, especially at the same time, when it can be avoided. The strange sight, on occasions when many priests are gathered together, of all of them offering separate masses and quietly ignoring each other (and often under conditions lacking a minimum of reverence or even decency!), must therefore disappear. It is a quite recent innovation and the product of a very inadequate (to say the least) realization of what the mass means. If it is a praiseworthy idea that every priest should celebrate mass as often as possible, the other idea, that to do so in such a way is normal, has nothing to do with it. Whenever separate masses are not required for separate gatherings of the faithful, the only normal, as well as the only traditional, way is concelebration. In concelebration, although only one priest presides at the eucharist, as the *locum tenens* of our Lord among us, all the other priests, sharing ministerially in the unique priesthood of Christ, are one with him in the consecration of sacrament and sacrifice. Therefore, the Council has solemnly decided that a rite for concelebration, in which that full participation will be achieved in a way both traditional and clearly expressive, is to be reintroduced in the Western Church, as it has ever been preserved in the Eastern. It means that it is no longer to be regarded by us as an extraordinary practice (used only now in the case of the mass for episcopal consecration or a priestly ordination). Here is exactly what the Council has decreed: "Concelebration, whereby the unity of the priesthood is appropriately manifested, has remained in use to this day in the Church, both in the East and in the West. For this reason it has seemed good to the Council to extend permission for concelebration to the following cases:

1. a) on the Thursday of the Lord's Supper, not only at the mass of the Chrism but also at the evening mass;

b) at masses during Councils, bishops' conferences, and synods;

c) at the mass for the blessing of an abbot.

2. Also, with the permission of the ordinary, to whom it belongs to decide when concelebration is opportune:

a) at conventual masses and at the principal mass in churches when the needs of the faithful do not require that all the priests available should celebrate individually;

b) at masses celebrated at any kind of priests' meetings, whether the priests be secular clergy or religious. The regulation, however, of the discipline of concelebration in the diocese pertains to the bishop" (par. 57).

One point is to be stressed here. Concelebration is especially desirable when priests meet with their bishop (as in a synod, or whenever he celebrates publicly), for it makes it clear that their priesthood is a sharing of his own priesthood. If they are his co-operators, then it is in the mass, above all, that it should become manifest. This is the reason why the Roman Pontifical—especially in what is said there about the Easter celebration in the cathedral—very forcefully expressed the view that it should be a matter of course that no priest would think of having his own separate celebration when the High Priest of the diocese solemnly pontificates.

For a different but no less imperative purpose, when bishops meet, as in a Council, it has always been traditional that they concelebrate, so as to make clear the unity of all the local churches in the Catholic Church, in and through the Eucharist. In this the collegiality of the episcopacy finds its most striking expression.

It may be noted that in the past a distinction was made between this concelebration of bishops and the concelebration of priests, either with their bishop or with a priest acting as his representative. In the first case, it was considered becoming that the equality of the concelebrants should be made manifest through the distribution between them, or the saying in common, of some of the essential prayers, usually said by the celebrant alone. In Christian antiquity, however, this was not done in the case of concelebrants of an inferior order, simply because their priesthood is only a derivation of that of the bishop. Nevertheless, the practice of the Church, as the Council has indicated, having found it desirable that all priests should frequently exercise their priesthood fully in the eucharist (as the bishop's representatives in the different parishes or among lesser groupings of the faithful), it has seemed desirable also that something of that should be introduced in every concelebration. Therefore, the new rite drafted by the post-conciliar commission, in accordance with the wish of the Council[14] provides for that, and the concelebration will render not only fully effective but fully manifest the fact that all the concelebrants consecrate together, under the leadership of the bishop and in cooperation with him.

Another most important detail concerning the liturgical celebration (and first of all the eucharistic celebration, considered as the achievement of this "sacrament of Unity" which is the mystery of the Church) is the re-establishment by the Council of communion under both species for all the Christian people.

"That more perfect form of participation in the mass whereby the faithful, after the priest's communion, receive the Lord's body from the same sacrifice, is strongly recommended.

"The dogmatic principles which were laid down by the Council of Trent remaining intact,[15]

---

[14] "A new rite for concelebration is to be drawn up and inserted into the Pontifical and into the Roman Missal" (par. 58).

[15] Session XXI, July 16, 1562. *Doctrine on Communion under both Species*, Chap. 1-3.

communion under both kinds may be granted when the bishops think fit, not only to clerics and religious, but also to the laity, in cases to be determined by the Apostolic See, as, for instance, to the newly ordained in the mass of their sacred ordination, to the newly professed in the mass of their religious profession, and to the newly baptized in the mass which follows their baptism" (par. 55).

The disappearance in the West of the communion under both kinds of anybody else (laity or not) than the celebrant happened progressively through the Middle Ages, by way of a custom which finally acquired a legal character. It was the fruit of both the practical difficulty of giving communion with the chalice to great assemblies, and a reverence for the sacred species which was not always well conceived (did not the practice result in practically a disappearance of a general communion at mass, until quite recently?). When the Protestants reacted against that use, the mind of the Church, at first, seemed ready to accept their protest on that point. It was only eventually rejected by the Council of Trent, primarily because the Protestant Reformers had mistakenly begun to teach that the Church (as they said) "had denied the cup to the laity" in order to reserve full communion to the priests alone. And there were also, among Catholics themselves at that time, some wrong ideas, as though the real

manducation of the eucharist was to be understood in a materialistic way. Therefore, the Council of Trent asserted that the real presence of the
Body and Blood of the now risen Lord was to be
understood in a spiritual way (which does not
mean less real for all that!), so that the entire humanity of the Savior, together with His divinity,
is received under even the least part of the sacramental species. But it is nevertheless true that
since the sacraments must express as fully as
possible their invisible reality in their visible sym-
bolism, the best form of the rite is one in which
the full participation of the people is completely
expressed. Therefore, without suddenly sup-
pressing a now very old custom, which surely
makes the administration of communion easier,
the Council suggests at least some limited reintroduction, to begin with, of the primitive practice. This will at least make clear that the participation of the laity in Holy Communion is as
complete as that of the clerics. The wisdom of the
reform introduced in such a moderate way is also
reflected in the decision of the Council concerning
concelebration, however desirable this may also
be: "Let each priest, nevertheless, retain his right
to celebrate the mass individually, though not at
the same time in the same church, nor on Thursday of the Lord's supper" (end of par. 57). What
is needed in both cases is a rediscovery of the full
meaning of the mass, which cannot be attained

simply through immediately compulsory deci-
sions, but rather through a progressive restoration. However, as the conclusion of the last
sentence quoted makes it imperative, practices
which are directly opposed to the true meaning
of the eucharist cannot be maintained any longer.
A priest may be allowed to celebrate individually,
so long as he has, or thinks he has, good reason
to do so, but that most objectionable practice,
forbidden by all the ancient tradition, of having
more than one mass at the same time in the same
church, is now to cease (let us hope for ever!).[16]

But the unity of the celebration and its communal character (since, in it, the Church itself is
built and manifested to the world in its unity)
must not be understood wrongly. It does not
mean that everybody is to do or to say everything together. In particular, a full participation
of the laity does not mean any obliteration of the
distinctive function of the apostolic ministry,
which is to preside at the eucharist and consecrate it in the name of Christ Himself. Nor does
a communal celebration mean an action so collective that the individual would have to disappear
into an anonymous mass. All those mistaken
views are directly opposed to St. Paul's descrip-

---

[16] Some translations err in this respect: the Council
does not say that private celebration is forbidden when
and where there is concelebration, but when and where
there is *any public mass*.

tion of the mystical body, wherein the apostle has so strongly affirmed that there are varieties of gifts and of ministries, while every gift and every ministry is to be exercised in harmony, for the common good. It is again what the Council teaches us, in a way which evokes the constant teaching of the early Fathers on so important a point, too often little comprehended or not understood at all today.

"In liturgical celebrations, each person, minister or layman, who has an office to perform, should do all of, but only, those parts which pertain to his office by the nature of the rite and the principles of liturgy" (par. 28).

If this is well understood, we should no longer see either masses where the people are reduced to the status of mere onlookers, or masses where the part of the priest is doubled by a commentator who attracts to himself all the attention, substituting his translations (or paraphrases!) for the genuine part of the priest, who is reduced to mumbling formulae intended to be public prayers *par excellence*. This last, quite recent deformation, which has so quickly reached such enormous dimensions, is a dead end out of which the liturgical movement has to be diverted as soon as possible. It has been introduced as necessary for people to follow a liturgy performed in a language now obsolete. But the reintroduction of the vernacular into the liturgy should suppress that supreme incongruity of taking from the priest his fundamental function of leader of the prayer. To have succeeded, rather, in making him accomplish his public role as a most private part, in the remote background of a pseudo-liturgy developing independently, is certainly a frightful failure issuing from too many so-called liturgical innovations. If it were to last, it would mean simply the death of the true liturgy. Nothing else but the vernacular could save us from that mortal contradiction.

We need not say that a no less patent aberration, condemned here in the most definite terms, is another practice, an equally recent, ill-understood device to make people participate: the collective recitation by all (usually in the vernacular) of the priestly prayers, and especially of the canon. Here we find the extreme confusion which may arise from a wrong interpretation of the idea that the Mass is a public or collective function. The priesthood of the laity, or, more exactly, of the whole people of God, cannot mean or even seem to mean that the laity could or should all together assume the part of the ministerial-priesthood. This is nothing other than the erroneous idea of the common priesthood of the faithful which was introduced by the Protestant reformers, although no Protestant Church, so far as I know, has ever brought it to such a fantastic extremity. If the fundamental, biblical idea that the laity share in the priesthood of Christ became so obscured in the Catholic Church during the last centuries, it was the result of an unavoidable reaction against their mistake. If we are to recapture it now, therefore, we must beware of relapsing into the same absurdity, in a form so outrageous that no sect has even dared to introduce it.

Just in the line of thought re-expressed now by the Council, from the very beginning the Fathers had understood the priesthood of the laity to be exercised in the liturgy, especially in the mass, in some specific actions: to pray, to offer, to communicate. However, they made it no less definite that only the ministerial priesthood in the Church is entitled to announce the Word of God with authority, to lead the common prayers, and finally to utter the eucharistic prayer, and thus to consecrate the offering of the faithful, so that they might receive it again as the Body and Blood of their Savior. This, and this only, is the traditional practice, in which is expressed the common life of the Church as that of a body, in which every member has its own part to perform in and for the life of the whole. Only in such a way can it be understood both that the royal priesthood of the whole people of God is fully real (and not at all metaphorical, as it is said sometimes, in a most unfelicitous phrase)—is, in other words, a real participation in the priesthood of Christ Himself—and that only the apostolic ministry can make it so real, by bringing Christ the Head into direct and actual touch with His members gathered in unity.

The modes of expression for universal participation in the liturgy are also described by the Council in words which are all to be equally emphasized: "To promote active participation, the people should be encouraged to take part by means of acclamations, responses, psalmody, antiphons, and songs, as well as by actions, gestures and bodily attitudes. And at proper times all should observe a reverent silence" (par. 30).

This is most explicit on the necessity, for participation, of more than a pious and attentive assistance. The people participate by taking part, *their part*, of course, and a very full one. For it is of the essence of the liturgy to express (and even create) the most inner participation by visible, audible, materially active participation. However, once again, we have in the concluding words a very timely refutation of a too common and too current mistake. Too many enthusiastic devotees of the liturgical movement, whose lights are not equal to their zeal, have already provoked a dangerous reaction among the faithful, and especially among the best. A book like *Liturgy and Contemplation* by Jacques Maritain, even though it included some mistaken expressions as if the liturgy was something purely external, gave voice to some very serious and amply justified feelings. It is not by making people constantly stand up, sit down or kneel down, while shouting incessantly as soon as they are not talked to, that we shall make them participate. Public and collective prayer does not mean an exclusion of private and personal prayer. Far from it, it is intended to foster it, and that not only outside of the liturgy, before or after it, but in it. If people do not pray—and indeed, one doesn't pray if he doesn't do more than making his own the words of another: he has also to do it in his own words, or better still in a mode that passes beyond words—if people do not pray in the liturgy because an unceasing turmoil prevents them from doing it, then the liturgy, however noisy and agitated, has become interiorly dead.

Silence, thus, is an integral part of it. We must understand this not only with respect to the silent attention paid by the faithful to the prayers of the priest, especially in the Canon, but also of moments of silence when everyone must develop for himself, in his own way, the themes evoked by the liturgical text. The oldest liturgical tradition always included those silences, devoted to the most personal assimilation by the faithful of what they might have received from the liturgical texts. From the explanations of the Fathers, it is abundantly clear that when they mentioned prayer as the basic priestly action of all the faithful, they had in mind those prayers, primarily, which were to be pursued after the *oremus*, either before the Collect, or at the Offertory, or before the Postcommunion. The *oratio fidelium* of the Offertory itself, as the Council wants to reintroduce it, and as it was practiced in the *orationes sollemnes* (still used on Good Friday) in the Roman mass, was a succession of such silent prayers, following exhortations of the deacon to pray for all possible Christian intentions, and to be concluded every time by a priestly collect. All these silent prayers of the faithful were not at all considered as something at the margin of the liturgy—least of all as foreign to it—but as an indispensable part of it.

We shall have to come back later to many of these points. But it is time now to see how the liturgical celebration, so fully described and explained by the Council, still according to its teaching, is to be related to the other aspects of the life of the Church and of the Christians.

IV

THE SITUATION OF THE LITURGY IN THE LIFE OF THE CHURCH

THE PRECEDING SHOULD HAVE REMOVED ALL POSSIBLE doubts concerning the centrality of the liturgy in the life of the Church. But, precisely to keep for it this centrality, the liturgy must not be made everything, which would be equivalent to making it simply anything. The fact that the liturgy is made for the faithful, and not for those who are still outside of the Church, must be stressed especially. More exactly, it is only when they are brought to the threshold of the Church that the liturgy is opened to them, in the preparatory parts of the baptismal liturgy. To say this much means that it would be a misguided pastoral effort that would try to adapt the liturgy in such a way that even unbelievers could easily follow and understand it. This, indeed, would not be a healthy adaptation of the liturgy, but its destruction. It had to be underlined, for much confusion has already been introduced in many minds, and much disorder in the celebration, by attempts to distort the liturgy according to a mistaken view of what it should be. Some people have even tried to replace the traditional liturgy (the only one that has a right to this name!) by some more or less fanciful "liturgy of the future." The Council dispels these erroneous views by saying explicitly: "The sacred liturgy does not exhaust the entire activity of the Church. Before men can come to the liturgy they must be called to faith and to conversion: 'How then are they to call upon Him Whom they have not heard? And how are they to hear if no one preaches? And how are men to preach unless they be sent?' (Rom. 10:14-15).

"Therefore, the Church announces the good tidings of salvation to those who do not believe, so that all men may know the true God and Jesus Christ Whom He has sent, and may be converted from their ways, doing penance."[17]

In other words, properly missionary work is not the work of the liturgy. This work must be performed, in different ways, before the liturgy may be celebrated. It is not the liturgy but the preaching of the word of salvation which has to be adapted to unbelievers as such. However, this very adaptation of the missionary activities of the Church, and especially of her teaching, to those outside would itself be meaningless if they were not to be themselves adapted, in their turn, to the

---

[17] Cf. John 17:3; Luke 24:27; Acts 2:38.

life of the faithful. As the Council puts it a few lines later: "Nevertheless the liturgy is the summit towards which the activity of the Church is directed. . . ." And again: "For the aim and object of apostolic works is that all who are made sons of God by faith and baptism should come together to praise God in the midst of the Church, to take part in the sacrifice and to eat the Lord's supper" (par. 10).

One result of this is that the adaptation of the Church and her missionary work must be such as to eventually lead former unbelievers not merely to some abstract acceptance of the Christian belief, but to that life of the faith which is embodied in the liturgy. Therefore, preaching which will be truly missionary, whatever may be the need of expressing it in ways understandable and finally acceptable to the men of every time and every civilization, will also always have to prepare them not for a diluted or altered Christianity. It will, rather, be necessary to seek, from the very start, to orient them towards that full and pure realization of the Christian faith and the Christian life that is exhibited first of all in the traditional liturgy. If it is of the essence of apologetics to try to meet the objections or difficulties of the unbelievers, even the first preaching of the Gospel to them will have to go beyond that merely negative or preparatory approach. It will be moved by the impulse to attract them to a positive appreciation of the word of God, as is incessantly echoed in the liturgy. This word will have to be translated, explained, and above all progressively unfolded to them, as it was, indeed, in the making of the People of God out of the mass of mankind. But, from the first, it will be oriented around the plenitude which can be discovered only in the Church, through the full disclosure of the divine Word, in the very words chosen by God. Under all missionary adaptations, therefore, there must be a continuity preserved with that full and supreme expression which remains to be found finally in the liturgy itself. And that, far from making the task of preaching to unbelievers harder, will only make it easier. For there is no possible expression of the divine truth so fully human, so immediately susceptible of creating a positive response in any man, than that chosen by God Himself. The most crucial necessity here is that the missionaries themselves be so deeply imbued with it that they can express it in their own words, words able to touch the hearts and minds of any man. If they are so imbued, they will be spontaneously led to understand other men— their contemporaries—however remote they may be from the Gospel, and to sympathize with them so that they will make the divine message understandable and attractive, in its plenitude and authenticity. But if they are not so imbued, the best sociological or psychological approaches, and even the most skillful capacity to discuss objections, will prove unable to really bring men to God as revealed in Christ. The important thing here is to have grasped, in the liturgical experience, how the word of God is a word of life. This is not only what will be most effective in touching men's hearts, but also what will succeed in leading them to the very sanctuary of liturgical life.

What the Council says, therefore, on what is to come before the liturgy, in the activity of the Church, has to be complemented immediately by what it also says concerning what is to come after. We have already quoted these words: "Nevertheless, the liturgy is the summit towards which the activity of the Church is directed." Then follows: "At the same time it is the fount from which all her power flows. For the aim and object of apostolic words is that all who are made sons of God by faith and baptism should come together to praise God in the midst of His Church, to take part in the sacrifice and to eat the Lord's Supper.

"The liturgy in its turn moves the faithful, filled with 'the paschal sacraments,' to be 'one in holiness"; [18] it prays that 'they may hold fast in their lives to what they have grasped by their faith';[19] the renewal in the eucharist of the covenant between the Lord and man draws the faith-

---

[18] Postcommunion for Easter Sunday.
[19] Collect of the Mass for Tuesday of Easter Week.

ful and inflames them into the compelling love of Christ. From the liturgy, therefore, and especially from the eucharist, as from a fount, grace is poured forth upon us; and the sanctification of men in Christ and the glorification of God, to which all other activities of the Church are directed as towards their end, is achieved in the most efficacious possible way" (par 10).

It may be said, as a summary of that last paragraph, that the liturgy is to prolong itself in the whole life of every Christian and of the whole Church, and that that is achieved through charity. Conversely, that charity which is to overflow from the experience of the liturgical life, and especially of our participation in the eucharist, is to provide the apostolic ministry of the Church with its most powerful argument to convert unbelievers: the witness of Christian life, in individuals as well as in the Christian community. What better demonstration of the evangelical truth could be offered to the world than the charity exercised by Christians, first of all among themselves, and then by all together, as well as by everyone in particular towards all men? What could be a greater incentive for bringing all men into the eucharist celebration in which the Church builds herself into the body of Christ than such a visible effect on those who take part already?

Thus, what precedes and what follows the liturgy in the life of the Church join together. It is what flows from the fount of the liturgical life that must be most effective in bringing men to its summit. The missionary work of the apostolic ministry tends finally to produce, through the liturgical mystery, through the mystery of the Church, that demonstration of love which will become its own justification and prove its most powerful support.

However, even for the baptized Christians—especially today when so many are received early in the Church through baptism but later on have little realization of what it should imply—there is again need to be taught in the Christian truth and renovated in its necessary consequences. Therefore, to them also the Church must teach again and again the fundamental beliefs and preach penance. But, especially, she must provide all that as a renewed introduction to the spirit of the liturgy, so that the liturgy will become the best way to deepen their Christianity, even though it must be complemented by more elementary means of approach. As the Council says: "To believers also the Church must ever preach faith and penance; she must prepare them for the sacraments, teach them to observe all that Christ has commanded,[20] and invite them to all the works of charity, piety and the apostolate" (par. 9).

---

[20] Cf. Matthew 28:20.

It is in that way that the various devotions are to be kept and encouraged, in so far as they may become a preparation to the liturgy. But this means that they will be prevented from ever supplanting the liturgy itself; rather, they will be deliberately harmonized with its spirit.

"Popular devotions of the Christian people are to be highly commended, provided they accord with the laws and norms of the Church, above all when they are ordered by the Holy See. Devotions proper to individual churches also have a special dignity if they are undertaken by mandate of the bishops according to customs or books lawfully approved. But these devotions should be so drawn up that they harmonize with the liturgical seasons, accord with the sacred liturgy, are in some fashion derived from it, and lead the people to it, since, in fact, the liturgy by its very nature far surpasses any of them" (par. 13). This final declaration, so categorical that it needs no further comment, explains why the Council, before and above all the "particular devotions," emphasizes the need of that "devotion" (in the singular) which consists of making fully personal the prayer the Church has taught us and the sacrifice to which she has introduced us sacramentally.

"The spiritual life, however, is not limited solely to participation in the liturgy. The Christian is indeed called to pray with his brethren, but he must also enter his chamber to pray to the Father in secret;[21] yet more, according to the teaching of the apostle, he should pray without ceasing.[22] We learn from the same Apostle that we must always bear about in our body the dying of Jesus, so that also the life of Jesus may be made manifest in our bodily frame.[23] This is why we ask the Lord in the sacrifice of the Mass that, 'receiving the offering of the spiritual victim,' He may fashion us for Himself 'as an eternal gift' "[24] (par. 12).

We have said that even in the liturgy at the present time there is a real prayer only in so far as individual Christians make the collective prayer their own, which presupposes that there is already room for silence and personal meditation. Even more, the participation in the liturgical prayer must be seen not so much as the whole of our life of prayer, but rather as the impulse and nurture of that most personal prayer without which we cannot be really acceptable to God the Father. And, since Christ insisted on it, this supposes for each of us an entry into the secrecy of our inner chamber and the sanctuary of our own heart. No collective prayer can dispense with that most personal one, and the whole public prayer

---

[21] Cf. Matthew 6:6.
[22] Cf. I Thess. 5:17.
[23] Cf. II Cor. 4:10-11.
[24] Secret for Monday of Pentecost Week.

is to foster it. In the same way, our association with the sacrifice of Christ in the mass would be meaningless if it were not to prove its reality by our actual assumption of our cross, to follow Him in daily life. Only through personal sacrifice accompanying personal prayer will the public prayer and sacrifice of the Church shed forth in our hearts, by the power of the Spirit, the true love of God. Only then will all these extensions into actual life, in the life of every one of us and in every day, draw men to Christ and His mystery, by showing forth His wonderful grace. "For all these works make it clear that Christ's faithful, though not of this world, are to be the light of the world and to glorify the Father before men" (par. 9).

V

OBJECTIVE GIFT
AND SUBJECTIVE RECEPTION

SO THAT THE LITURGY MAY BEAR THE FRUIT WE HAVE just described, it must be realized in such a way that it will become alive for Christians, and first of all, it must be understood by them. As the Council puts it: "In order that the liturgy may be able to produce its full effects, it is necessary that the faithful come to it with proper dispositions, that their minds should be attuned to their voices, and that they should co-operate with divine grace, lest they receive it in vain.[25] Pastors of souls must therefore realize that, when the liturgy is celebrated, something more is required than the mere observation of the laws governing valid and licit celebrations; it is their duty to ensure that the faithful take part fully aware of what they are doing, actively engaged in the rite, and enriched by its effects" (par. 11).

Here we come to a point of the highest importance. If it is missed, no liturgical renewal will

---

[25] Cf. II Cor. 6:1.

be able to achieve anything of a lasting and substantial importance. In the controversies with
the Protestant reformers, the emphasis has been
put on what they were all more or less losing sight
of: the efficacy of the sacraments *ex opere oper-
ato*. And it is certainly a basic truth that divine
grace is given to us through the sacramental action, as soon as it is validly and licitly performed,
in a way which does not depend on our dispositions but only on the sovereign power of God,
who has freely attached His gifts to the signs
of them given by Christ. Nonetheless, the objective gift of grace will remain unfruitful if it
is not received with the proper disposition, and,
first of all, with a faith rightly and fully devel-
oped. However this, even where it has not been
forgotten, has been sought for by means which,
for generations, had little or nothing to do with
the liturgy. The liturgy was sometimes celebrated
with great dignity, as was thought befitting to the
presence within it of powerful gifts of grace, but
no attention was paid to what it included which
had been originally intended as a means of making us aware of those gifts, and of opening us to
their influence. To a strict observance of the rubrics might be added an exterior solemnity, but
that was all. The assimilation of sacramental
grace was expected from all kinds of devotions,
more or less foreign to the liturgy and to its spirit.
Few thought that the liturgy itself, if celebrated

not only in a "correct" but in an intelligent way, provided for it. This strange divorce is the principal error which must be corrected in order to have a true restoration of the liturgy. Its unique value begins from the fact that in it the objective gift of God, in the sacramental action, is combined in the most organic way with the means most adequate to its proper subjective reception. However, this cannot be felt unless we take seriously the concrete problem of achieving what the Council calls, again and again, a "full, conscious and active participation."

"Mother Church earnestly desires that all the faithful should be led to that full, conscious and active participation in liturgical celebrations which is demanded by the very nature of the liturgy. Such participation by the Christian people as 'a chosen race, a royal priesthood, a holy nation, a redeemed people' (I Pet. 2:9; cf. 2:4-5) is their right and duty by reason of their baptism.

"In the restoration and promotion of the sacred liturgy, this full and active participation by all the people is the aim to be considered before all else; for it is the primary and indispensable source from which the faithful are to derive the true Christian spirit; and therefore, pastors of souls must zealously strive to achieve it, by means of the necessary instruction, in all their pastoral work" (par. 14).

It will be noticed that the sentence on a true

participation considered as "the primary and indispensable source from which the faithful are
to derive the true Christian spirit" is a quotation
from the famous *Motu Proprio* of St. Pius X,
which Dom Lambert Beauduin had made the
motto of the liturgical movement in Belgium.
Now, while he had been repeatedly accused of
inflating and perverting the meaning of that sentence, the Council makes his interpretation its
own in the most uncompromising way.

The Council especially consecrates the basic
notion that the instruction needed to worship
properly is provided in worship itself, in an irre-
placeable manner. That other sentence of Pius XI
(which, not long ago, I heard some priests call a
most unfortunate statement), "the liturgy is the
main organ of the ordinary magisterium of the
Church," could be quoted as a summary of one
of the most important parts of the Conciliar Constitution.

"Although the sacred liturgy is above all things
the worship of the divine Majesty, it likewise
contains much instruction for the faithful.[26] For
in the liturgy God speaks to His people and Christ
is still proclaiming His Gospel. And the people
reply to God both by song and prayer.

"Moreover, the prayers addressed to God by
the priest who presides over the assembly in the

---

[26] Cf. Council of Trent, Session XXII, Doctrine on the
Holy Sacrifice of the Mass, c.8.

person of Christ are said in the name of the entire holy people and of all present. And the visible
signs used by the liturgy to signify invisible divine things have been chosen by Christ or the
Church. Thus not only when things are read
'which were written for our instruction' (Rom.
15:4), but also when the Church prays or sings or
acts, the faith of those taking part is nourished
and their minds are raised to God, so that they
may offer Him their rational services and more
abundantly receive His grace" (par. 33).

One of the most spectacular revisions of the
liturgy springing explicitly from these principles
will be the wider introduction of the vernacular,
especially in the mass.

"Particular law remaining in force, the use of
the Latin language is to be preserved in the Latin
rites. But since the use of the mother tongue,
whether in the Mass, the administration of the
sacraments, or other parts of the liturgy, frequently may be of great advantage to the people,
the limits of its employment may be extended.
This will apply in the first place to the readings
and directives, and to some of the prayers and
chants, according to the regulations on this matter to be laid down separately in subsequent chapters" (par. 36).

It is, indeed, a plain matter of common sense
that readings in the liturgy, being directly and
exclusively intended for the instruction of the

people, should be in a language understood by
them. It is merely painful evidence of the sad
power of routine (mistaken for tradition) that it
could have been forgotten for such a long time.
And, as the Council has indicated, this should
also be admitted as a matter of fact concerning
the variable chants and prayers connected with
the readings. Actually, this could surely have
been achieved centuries ago, if the Protestant
Reformation had not most unfortunately combined the translation of all these parts of the
liturgy with drastic changes, leading to more or
less a complete break with tradition.

However, as the Council also expresses it, we
should not, for that reason, suppose that the vernacular must be introduced everywhere in the
liturgy, nor, still less, that it would suffice to make
the liturgy perfectly understandable.

On the first point, it must be said before all
that a canonical text of the prayers of the Church,
in their traditional form, must be kept as a common basis for all the translations. It is such an
obvious necessity that it has been felt by practically all the churches influenced by the Protestant
Reformation which have not completely lost a
sense of tradition. The first and basic Lutheran
liturgy, in Germany, was the *Formula Missae* of
Luther, which he wrote in Latin and insisted
should be kept in that language, at least in col-
leges, for the benefit, especially, of candidates to

the priesthood. The same holds true of the Swedish liturgy, and Cranmer himself, although he was probably the most skillful author of a modern vernacular liturgy, was very careful to produce a standard edition of his prayer book in traditional Latin. It may be of interest to note that the Church of England (Anglican) has recently decided that the use of that text should be revived, at least in some collegiate churches. To dispense altogether with the Latin in worship would mean, for the priests who are to have a first-hand familiarity with the Christian tradition, a very serious loss, for it would mean their estrangement from all the sources of Christian culture in the West.

However even for parochial celebrations, it is not so clear, as some seem to believe, that the Latin should be simply suppressed. The great eucharistic prayer, which in the Western tradition remains always substantially the same, must and can become familiar to every Christian, with the use of translations properly explained. When it has, it is certainly a great advantage to follow the Church's most important act of worship in the very words which have been used by our forefathers since at least the third century. The same, as the Council expressly mentions, may be said of the five great hymns of the ordinary of the mass. It is very easy, even for people with little education, to get to know and understand

them, and it would be a pity if they could no
longer be sung in the Catholic Church in their
traditional musical setting of Gregorian chant,
when some Lutheran churches have still retained
them in that ancient form (see par. 54).

Just as a fanatical and exclusive attachment to
Latin may be unreasonable and opposed to the
good of souls, so, a desire to suppress any possible use of an ancient language appears equally
unreasonable. While archaism must never blind
us to real needs, we should not for that reason
forget that a ritual should never be forced into
the rigid pattern of contemporaneity. It is a part
of Christian ritual, as of any ritual, that it links
us with a multi-secular experience, and if we
would not accept this we should discard, as well,
not only practically everything in our rites, but
even the use of the Bible. It is a fact too often
neglected that our Lord Himself always wor-
shipped according to the ritual of the Palestinian
synagogue, in which only the readings, with a
few prayers immediately connected with them,
were in the vernacular. The great fixed prayers,
however, for the recital of the Shema, the Eigh-
teen benedictions, and the berakah for the last cup
of the meal (which are the three main sources of
our eucharistic prayers) were all retained in Hebrew, a language at least as dead then, so far as
common usage was concerned, as Latin is now.
If our Lord had found such a practice intolerable,

He who so relentlessly denounced the formalism of the Pharisees would certainly not have accepted that practice without a word of criticism, as He did.

The phobia for any Latin, which has suddenly achieved, in some liturgical circles, an almost incredible attachment to its exclusive use, is most of the time based on the naive assumption that the barrier of language is the only obstacle to a full and easy understanding of the liturgy. To tell the truth, the gradual disappearance of Latin will only make easier the effort of explaining, and above all the unavoidable task of re-creating, a religious culture too often completely lost. Whatever may be the importance of a wider use of the vernacular, the Council is certainly correct in emphasizing, far more, the absolute necessity of an initiation to the Bible. Not only because the Bible provides us with the readings given in the liturgy, but because it has directly inspired the whole of it, the liturgy will never again become the familiar prayer of the Christians if the Bible remains for them as a sealed book, which it still is, unfortunately, not only for the majority of them, but for too many priests. And it would be a complete betrayal of authentic Christianity to dream of a new liturgy where that could cease to be the truth. To give us the word of God, in its primitive and directly inspired expression, is the basic aim of any liturgy worthy of the name.

Therefore the Council suggests, far from reducing the liturgical use of Scripture, to make it again as extensive as it was in primitive Christianity, while insisting on the fundamental task of the clergy to initiate the faithful to its proper interpretation and to make them again truly familiar with it.

"Sacred scripture," says the Council, "is of the greatest importance in the celebration of the liturgy. For it is from Scripture that lessons are read and explained in the homily, and psalms are sung; the prayers, collects and liturgical songs are scriptural in their inspiration, and it is from the scriptures that actions and signs derive their meaning. Thus, to achieve the restoration, progress and adaptation of the sacred liturgy, it is essential to promote that warm and living love for scripture to which the venerable tradition of both eastern and western rites gives testimony" (par. 24).

All this may be summarized to say that the basis for any initiation to the liturgy is an initiation to the Bible. And since the best way to understand the Bible—which is a whole world of thought, wonderfully varied but no less wonderfully connected into a living unity—is to become familiar with it, the first decision of the Council on this point is to reopen, as abundantly as possible, the treasures of Scripture to the whole people of God. At the same time, the Council enjoins

the clergy to take care not only to preach at the
liturgical celebrations, but to give their people a
real homily, which means a commentary on the
texts read, applying their coherent meaning to the
spiritual life of the faithful.

"That the intimate connection between words
and rites may be apparent in the liturgy:

"1) In sacred celebration, there is to be more
reading from holy scripture, and it is to be more
varied and suitable" (par. 35). This points to the
revision of the lectionary for both the missal and
the breviary, which has been undertaken by the
post-conciliar commission. For the missal, it
should revive the reading of the Old Testament
(now most of the time absent from the Roman
rite, although still retained in every mass at
Milan, in the so-called Ambrosian rite, more
faithful on this point as on others to the oldest
Roman tradition). But it should also include, especially for the Sundays after Epiphany and after
Pentecost, two'or more series of alternative readings of epistles and gospels, together with provision for daily celebrations throughout the whole
year. In the breviary it should provide a rational
selection of the main texts of each biblical book,
giving the essentials at least of their message.

"2) Because the sermon is part of the liturgical
service, the best place for it is to be indicated even
in the rubrics, so far as the nature of the rite will
allow; the ministry of preaching is to be fulfilled

with exactitude and fidelity. The sermon, moreover, should draw its content mainly from scriptural and liturgical sources, and its character
should be that of a proclamation of God's wonderful works in the history of salvation, the mystery of Christ, ever made present and active
within us, especially in the celebration of the
liturgy" (*ibid.*).

This restoration of preaching to its place in the
liturgy, as an essential part of it, defines also what
a real sermon should be. Since it is not an inter-
ruption of the liturgy, but organically one with it,
it cannot be simply any kind of religious instruction. It must be a direct commentary, first of the
biblical texts read, in their whole liturgical context, i.e., together with an explanation of the
prayers and the rites, so that the actuality of the
word of God may be realized for the congregation
which hears it. What the sermon must always
tend to do is to bring the people to enter into the
history of salvation, by revealing to them the
presence of the mystery of Christ as manifested
by the liturgy. If it does not do this, it is not a
sermon at all, even if it is a fine lesson in
theology, in religious history, or in Christian
ethics.

"3) Instruction which is more explicitly liturgical should also be given in a variety of ways; if
necessary, short directives to be spoken by the
priest or proper minister should be provided

within the rites themselves. But they should occur only at the more suitable moments, and be in prescribed or similar words" (*ibid.*).

Apart from the sermon itself, this requires, as a part of any Christian teaching, a general and detailed initiation into the rites and their significance. But the words used by the Council (not with respect to that general teaching, nor the sermon itself) regarding the "commentaries" which have become so frequent (and too often superabundant) in recent years, are expressing a much needed caution. Such commentaries might be necessary when there was no use of the vernacular in the liturgy, or when the sermon, all too commonly, had nothing to do with the liturgy. When these two defects have been corrected, the need for commentaries will be much reduced. Then they will have to be maintained in the liturgy only in special cases (in the case of an extraordinary function with which the faithful may not be familiar, like the consecration of a church, or, perhaps, an ordination). But it is essential that they do not interrupt the liturgical action, and above all that they do not destroy the atmosphere of prayer, nor substitute a running and loose teaching (as is too often the case) and confronted with which the faithful remain passive, for their real participation. This supposes, first, that the commentary be given either by the celebrating priest or his minister (a deacon if possible, of course), and that it be always short, at the right place, and with a severe restraint.

However, the Council does not content itself with demanding a fuller use of scripture and a better initiation to it in the context of the rites as we have them now, especially the mass. It encourages a return to the practice of scriptural services, common in the ancient church, especially on the vigils of the great feasts, as well as on weekdays in Lent and Advent, and on Sundays and feast days. It even goes so far as to suggest their celebration under the leadership of a deacon, or of any other person authorized by the bishop, in places where no priest is available (*ibid*. n. 4).

This point emphasizes more strikingly than anything else how much—for the Council—initiation to a "full," and, even prior to that, a "conscious," celebration of the liturgy means a restored familiarity with the word of God, so that our prayer may become, as it always is in the liturgy, a response to it. However, what will be the fully "active" participation (not only in the prayer of the church, but in the liturgical action *par excellence*, i.e., in the presence of Christ's mystery, on these bases) is better described in the program for the restoration of the eucharistic celebration, which will bring us to the end of our study. There, indeed, if ever, we will participate, not only by a right understanding of what is taking place, but in a prayer which leads to self-surrender to the presence of Christ and takes us into the most sacred mystery of our salvation.

"At the last supper, on the night when He was betrayed, our Savior instituted the eucharistic sacrifice of His body and blood. He did this in order to perpetuate the sacrifice of the Cross throughout the centuries until He should come again, and so to entrust to His beloved spouse, the Church, a memorial of His death and resurrection: a sacrament of love, a sign of unity, a bond of charity,[27] a paschal banquet in which Christ is eaten, the mind is filled with grace, and a pledge of future glory is given to us.[28]

"The Church, therefore, earnestly desires that Christ's faithful, when present at this mystery of faith, should not be there as strangers or silent spectators; on the contrary, through a good understanding of the rites and prayers they should take part in the sacred action conscious of what they are doing, with devotion and full collaboration. They should be instructed by God's word and be nourished at the table of the Lord's body; they should give thanks to God; by offering the immaculate victim, not only through the hands of the priest, but also with him, they should learn also to offer themselves; through Christ the me-

---

[27] Cf. St. Augustine, *Tractatus in Joannem*, VI, n.13.

[28] Roman Breviary, Feast of Corpus Christi, Second Vespers, antiphon to the Magnificat.

diator,[29] they should be drawn day by day into ever more perfect union with God and with each other, so that finally God may be all in all" (par. 47-48).

This gives us the most perfect expression of what should be that "full, conscious and active participation" which is the aim of the whole Constitution. First, men must hear the word of God, attaining its plenitude in the Word made man and His sacrifice on the Cross. Then they should pray in answer to that word: giving thanks to God for His wonderful mystery. And finally they should be attracted to it, in the celebration of the everlasting sacrifice, offered once and for all on the Cross, and now offered sacramentally, so that we may be all together offered in it and become one, in the One Mediator, reconciled to God the Father, reconciled between us, in the body of His Son made man.

The whole plan for the revision of the eucharistic liturgy follows, dominated by these perspectives. So that the word of God be heard in its fullness, once again the Council decrees, with new precisions: "The treasures of the Bible are to be opened up more lavishly, so that richer fare may be provided for the faithful at the table of God's word."

---

[29] Cf. St. Cyril of Alexandria, *Commentary on the Gospel of John*, book XI, chap. XI-XII; Migne, *Patrologia graeca*, 74, 557-564.

Let us notice here the parallel so often drawn by the Fathers of the early Church, between that table of the spoken word, which is to nourish our faith, and the table of the incarnate word which nourishes our whole being.

"In this way, a more representative portion of the holy scriptures will be read to the people in the course of a prescribed number of years.

"By means of the homily the mysteries of faith and the guiding principles of the Christian life are expounded from the sacred text during the course of the liturgical year; the homily, there-fore, is to be highly esteemed as part of the lit-urgy itself; in fact, at those masses which are celebrated with the assistance of the people, on Sundays and feasts of obligation, it should not be omitted except for a serious reason. . . .

"The two parts which, in a certain sense, go to make up the mass, namely, the liturgy of the word and the eucharistic liturgy, are so closely con-nected with each other that they form but a single act of worship. Accordingly this sacred Synod strongly urges the pastors of souls that, when instructing the faithful, they insistently teach them to take their part in the entire mass, espe-cially on Sundays and feasts of obligation" (par. 51, 52, 56).

Then the Council prescribes a restoration of the "common prayer," or "prayer of the faith-ful," after the homily, so that we may be led to

the eucharistic prayer and sacrifice by a general
intercession "for all mankind and for the salvation of the entire world" (par. 53).

But it is in the section on the sacraments that
the Constitution gives us its final word on that
entrance into the reality of the mystery which
is to be achieved through a right understanding
of the whole meaning of the liturgy. There we
can see at last how the participation in the liturgy
is nothing else but the reception by a living faith
—illuminated and inflamed through the liturgy
itself—of the sacramental grace.

"The purpose of the sacraments is to sanctify
men, to build up the body of Christ, and, finally,
to give worship to God; because they are signs,
they also instruct. They not only presuppose
faith, but by words and objects (*verbis et rebus*)
they also nourish, strengthen and express it; that
is why they are called 'sacraments of faith.' They
do indeed impart grace, but, in addition, the very
act of celebrating them most effectively disposes
the faithful to receive this grace in a fruitful manner, to worship God duly and to practice charity"
(par. 59).

If a word of conclusion should be added to this
study of the doctrinal contents of the Conciliar
constitution, it should certainly be the solemn
warning of the Council to priests, as given below:

"It would be futile to entertain any hopes of

realizing this unless the pastors themselves, in the first place, become thoroughly imbued with the spirit and the power of the liturgy . . ." (par. 14). The liturgy is not a kind of new trick, to be used just as any other pastoral device, to galvanize artificially the lives of the faithful. Those who are to make people live by it are to be the first to do it for themselves. We cannot be the priests of a religion of which we are not truly the faithful.

The Notre Dame Pocket Library

A new paperback series, attractively produced, popularly priced.

PL-1   *Four Saints*. Louis Lavelle (translated by Dorothea O'Sullivan) . $.95

PL-2   *Individuation. A Study of the Depth Psychology of Carl Gustav Jung*. Josef Goldbrunner (translated by Stanley Godman) . . $.95

PL-3   *The Problem of Population, Moral and Theological Considerations*. Donald N. Barrett, ed. . . . $.95

PL-4   *Saint Bonaventure*. Efrem Bettoni (translated by Angelus Gambatese, O.F.M.) . . . . . . $.95

PL-5   *Holiness Is Wholeness and Other Essays*. Josef Goldbrunner . . $.95

PL-6   *The Problem of Population, Practical Catholic Applications*. Donald N. Barrett, ed. . . . $.95

PL-7   *The Use of Parables in Catechetics*. Franz Mussner . . . $.95

PL-8   *Christ and the End of the World. A Biblical Study in Eschatology*. Franz Mussner . . . . . $.95

PL-9   *Cure of Mind, Cure of Soul: Depth Psychology and Pastoral Care*. Josef Goldbrunner . . . . $.95

PL-10 *The Liturgy Revived*. Louis Bouyer . . . . $.95